Cats

Victoria Blakemore

For my students, who have been a source of ideas and inspiration, as well as Maggie's biggest fans.

© 2018 Victoria Blakemore

All rights reserved. This book or parts thereof may not be reproduced in any form, stored in any retrieval system, or transmitted in any form by any means—electronic, mechanical, photocopy, recording, or otherwise—without prior written permission of the publisher, except as provided by United States of America copyright law. For permission requests, write to the publisher, at "Attention: Permissions Coordinator," at the address below.

vblakemore.author@gmail.com

Copyright info/picture credits

Cover, Victoria Blakemore; Page 3, R-Fdesign/Pixabay; Page 5, Victority/Shutterstock; Page 7, Eric Isselée/AdobeStock; Page 9, rihaij/Pixabay; Pages 10-11, Quangpraha/Pixabay; Page 13, skeeze/Pixabay; Page 15, Alexas_Fotos/Pixabay; Page 17, rhaijj/Pixabay; Page 19, Kessa/Pixabay; Page 21, Anamaria Todor/Shutterstock; Page 23, rihaij/Pixabay; Page 25, CALLALLOO CANDCY/AdobeStock; Page 27, Storyblocks; Page 29, Kapa65/Pixabay; Page 31, Jakub Zak/Shutterstock; Page 33, Victoria Blakemore; Page 35, Victoria Blakemore

Table of Contents

What are Cats? 2

History 4

Cat Breeds 6

Physical Characteristics 8

Kittens 10

Diet 12

Hunting 14

Communication 16

Movement 18

Senses 20

Staying Clean 22

Intelligence 24

Getting a Pet Cat 26

Taking Care of Your Cat 28

Helping Cats 32

Glossary 36

What Are Cats?

Cats are small mammals. The cats we keep as pets are related to the African wild cat.

There are over 95 million pet cats in the United States, making them the most popular pet. Cats are also a popular pet in parts of Europe and the Middle East.

Domesticated cats are cats that are kept by humans. They are not wild cats or **feral** cats.

History

Cats were first kept by humans thousands of years ago in the Middle East. They were **sacred** to ancient Egyptians, who kept them to hunt mice.

Cats spread to other parts of the Middle East and Europe. They kept food free from rats and mice.

When explorers came to America, cats came across on their ships. They helped settlers keep their homes and crops free from pests.

Cat Breeds

There are many different breeds of cats. They differ in color, kind of coat, size, physical characteristics, and **temperament**.

Most pet cats are a mixture of breeds. They may have features from those different breeds.

Different breeds of cats come from different parts of the world.

Physical Characteristics

Most cats have thick fur. It can help to keep them warm. Some cats, like the rex, do not have fur. It is harder for them to stay warm.

Most cats have a long tail. Their tail can be used to communicate and can help them balance.

Cat whiskers help them to sense things that are around them. They also help cats to know if they can fit through or into something.

Kittens

Cats often have a **litter** of between four and six kittens. They usually weigh less than four ounces.

When they are first born, their eyes are closed and they cannot hear. They will be able to see and hear within about two weeks.

Kittens are born with blue eyes. Their eyes will change to their true color after about eight weeks.

Diet

Pet cats are often fed dry kibble, wet food, or a mixture of both. They both have protein, which gives cats energy.

Whichever food they are given, it is important that cats are not **overfed**. Cats that are overfed can get to be too heavy and have health problems.

Cats have sharp, strong teeth. Eating crunchy food helps to keep their teeth clean.

Hunting

Wild cats and **feral** cats need to hunt for their own food. They use their speed and strength to help them catch their prey.

Animals that cats hunt include birds, rats, mice, grasshoppers, frogs, lizards, and other small animals.

When cats are hunting, they often crouch down and sneak up on their prey.

Communication

Cats use movement, sound, and scent to communicate. They have a special scent that they rub on people and objects they feel that they own.

Pet cats that want something may meow at their owner. When a cat purrs, it is feeling safe and content.

Cats that have an **arched** back and puffed up fur may be afraid. They can growl or hiss if they are angry.

Movement

Cats can run very fast for short distances. They can run up to twenty-nine miles per hour. Cats are also very **agile**. They are able to turn quickly, even when they are running.

Cats spend most of their time sleeping. They can sleep over sixteen hours per day.

Cats have long claws that help them to climb. They often feel safe in high places.

Senses

Cats use their senses to help them move around at night. Their whiskers help them to sense what is around them.

The pupil is the dark part in the middle of the eye. It lets light in. A cats pupils **dilate**, or get larger, when it is dark so they can see.

A cats pupils can also dilate when they are hunting or about to pounce.

Staying Clean

Cats have a very rough tongue. They use it like a brush when they lick their fur.

The main purpose of this is to keep their coat clean and free from tangles. It can also help them to cool down and soothe them when they are stressed.

Cats wash their face by licking their paw. Once it is wet, they wipe it over their face.

Intelligence

Cats have been found to have very good memories. They can remember things and people years later.

They are very curious. They like to explore their space and finding new places to hide.

Some people teach their cats how to do tricks like standing on their **hind** legs or giving a high five.

Getting a Pet Cat

Before you get a pet cat, you need to make sure that you can take care of it. Having a cat is a big responsibility.

You should make sure you have the cat food, bowls, litter box, and litter. You will also need a cat carrier to get your cat home safely.

Many people adopt their cat at a shelter. Doing that helps cats that are in need of a home.

Taking Care of Your Cat

Cats need to be fed only cat food. They should not be given human food. It can make them sick.

Many people think that cats drink milk, but it can make their stomach sick. They should be given fresh water every day.

Cats, especially young cats and kittens, can be very playful and energetic. They need toys to play with. Cats that are bored could become **destructive**.

Cats need a litter box. It needs to be cleaned regularly. Scratching posts are also good to have. They give cats a safe place to scratch.

Pet cats should be taken to the vet yearly for their shots and a check-up. The vet can make sure that your cat stays healthy.

Although cats **groom** themselves, brushing your cat helps to get rid of extra fur. It can keep their fur from getting tangled and from making a mess in your house.

Helping Cats

Animal shelters are full of animals like cats that need a home. Many people choose to adopt from a shelter instead of buying a cat.

Some people take care of pets in their home until they find a forever home.

Some groups rescue pets that need help. They try to find them homes where they will be taken care of.

Some people who can't adopt a pet help by **volunteering** at shelters. They also **donate** things like pet food, towels, and blankets to shelters.

Glossary

Agile: moving quickly and gracefully

Arched: curved

Destructive: destroying things

Dilate: to expand and get larger

Domesticated: animals that are kept as pets and used to living with humans

Donate: to give something to help others

Feral: animals that are mostly wild, they may live in places around humans, but not with them

Groom: to make clean and neat

Hind: back

Litter: a group of animals born at the same time

Overfed: given too much food

Sacred: shown great respect

Temperament: the way a person or animal thinks and behaves

Volunteering: doing work to help, not for pay

About the Author

Victoria Blakemore is a first grade teacher. She lives in Southwest Florida with her cat, Maggie, who you might recognize from the cover!

You can visit Victoria at

www.elementaryexplorers.com

Also in This Series

Also in This Series

www.ingramcontent.com/pod-product-compliance
Lightning Source LLC
Chambersburg PA
CBHW042000080526
44588CB00021B/2814